Public Speaking for Executives, Leaders and Managers

John Zehring

Contents

INTRODUCTION

You have to give a speech. You want to do your best. You desire for your talk to be well received by your audience. You are also extremely busy, so need a brief aid to help you master the most important basics of public speaking quickly. You have witnessed public speaking done poorly. How can you avoid making some of the same mistakes? That is the purpose of _Public Speaking for Executives, Leaders and Managers_ – to give you a brief overview and key tips to help you prepare.

There are two parts to speeches: CONTENT and DELIVERY. Some prepare well, research, wrestle with the topic, connect the message to the audience, and deliver excellent information. For their content, they get an A+. The same speaker, on the other hand, may rate a C- on delivery. Perhaps the speaker does not make eye contact. Listeners do not feel seen. The speaker does not even peek at you when he or she speaks, let alone linger in a gaze that causes you to feel like you and he/she are engaged in a conversation. She reads most of her speech. Perhaps ninety percent of the time his eyes are affixed upon the paper on the podium. She stares out the side window as though watching the traffic. If you can see behind the podium, he is making a few hand gestures, but they are mostly to himself, not to aid in the delivery. His and her messages are still valuable. Better to have great content with inadequate delivery than the other way around. Who would favor all sizzle and no steak?

Why not master both content and delivery? This eBook aims to provide you with increased ability to connect with your audience. It will help you to self-evaluate your content and delivery to identify where more attention is needed.

Included is a self-evaluation checklist which you can apply to your speeches, which is adapted from the checklist I used when teaching public speaking at a university. The entire class used the checklist to evaluate each speaker. How would you like to stand before an audience rating each aspect of your content and delivery? Each speaker employed the checklist to evaluate him/herself. As the professor I used the checklist (along with the checklists from the class members) to determine a grade. When I spoke publically, I used the same checklist, painful as it was.

Public speakers receive feedback after each presentation. Almost always, it is positive in some way. It is rare for listeners to give a critical analysis of your work. So, you and I can be fooled into grading our work more highly than we should based upon the number of people who say *"Good speech."* This eBook is for leaders and executives who are motivated to want more and who desire to be first rate speakers in both content and delivery.

I will be honored if this work guides you in your continued improvement as a public speaker.

John Zehring

CHAPTER ONE: Ten Key Rules for Public Speaking

My wife's grandfather earned his living as an architectural renditionist. Before computers were in use, he would draw a rendition of what the architect's plans would look like when completed. By avocation, he was an artist who drew scenes of Philadelphia's Independence Hall, Williamsburg's Governor's Palace and of Maine's Friendship Harbor. I asked him if he ever delved into modern art. He told me that he was not yet good enough to paint modern art, because an artist must first master the rules before breaking them. Picasso, he added, was first taught by his father, Professor Ruiz, who believed that proper training required disciplined copying of the masters. Picasso was capable of forging the Old Masters before he broke the rules to depict a new way of seeing. So too with public speaking: first master the rules. Break them not until you

know what you are doing and why. Now,
the rules:

One: Write for the ear.
A danger is that what you write may end
up like something to be read rather than to
be heard. When you prepare for a speech,
what do you do? You go to your keyboard
and compose. You write it out. But that is
writing, usually to be read. Consider the
difference between writing a story for a
newspaper and writing the same for the
radio. It is a different style of writing.
People read the newspaper but listen to the
radio. Likewise, people listen to your
speech. So, a speech must be written for
the ear, not the eye.

When writing a message, talk it out loud as
you write to see how it sounds to you.
Imagine how it will be heard by your
listeners. Rehearse it out loud before
delivering it. Commandment number one:
write for the ear, not for the eye.

Two: Make every word tell.
This comes from one of the greatest style manuals ever written. In *The Elements of Style* by William Strunk, Jr. and E. B. White, one of the utmost pieces of advice to writers ever given is this:

Vigorous writing is concise. A sentence should contain no unnecessary words, a paragraph no unnecessary sentences, for the same reason that a drawing should have no unnecessary lines and a machine no unnecessary parts. This requires not that the writer make all his sentences short, or that he avoid all detail and treat his subjects only in outline, but that every word tell.

Strunk and White's counsel is to omit needless words. All writing should be clear, plain, active and concise. When writing for the ear, clear and concise writing is cherished by listeners.

In a speech, it is the power of language that grabs listeners. Think of great speeches you have heard and how the speakers moved people by their words. What counted most? It was not necessarily eye contact, important as that is: Winston Churchill did not make eye contact. It was not that the speaker looked too much at notes: Nelson Mandela hardly looked up from his written manuscript. It was not the length of the speech: Ronald Regan's eulogy to the Challenger astronauts captured in fifty one seconds what it might take many of us fifteen minutes to say and we could never say it so eloquently.

Winston Churchill said *"Short words are best and the old words when short are best of all."* Plato, Lincoln, Jesus, and Martin Luther King, Jr. employed mostly words of one or two syllables. Lincoln's Gettysburg Address contains 271 words and all but twenty are only one or two syllables. Favor short words, short sentences, and active verbs. Consider some classic lines:

These are the times that try men's souls

It was the best of times, it was the worst of times.

Two roads diverged into a yellow wood... and I took the one less traveled by.

Ask not what your country can do for you...

I have a dream...

The Lord is my shepherd, I shall not want.

To be, or not to be, that is the question.

Do you notice the obvious? Most are short words of one or two syllables. When you invest your effort to craft the message and weave the words together, your audience will be grateful, will remember, and will be moved because listeners appreciate outstanding communication. Make every word tell.

11

Three: Use *"you"* words.

The first person singular is the pronoun cherished by listeners: *I, me* or *mine*. We like those and use them most. Are not most listeners drawn in by the word *"me"*? From the podium, the word *"you"* has the same effect: it is well received and causes the listener to pay careful attention because *"the speaker is talking to me."* When you use the word *"you"* in public speaking, use it in the singular, not the plural. That is, speak to *"you"* as an individual, not to *you* as a group of people… *"you people."* Speaking to *"you all"* loses the impact of speaking to one person… to me. Consider: *"I am glad you are here today"* makes it sound like you are glad I am present. *"I am glad you are all here today"* makes me just one of a bunch, noticed or not.

Unlearn the use of the word *"one"* when referring to a person. That might have been a favored style for college papers, but

12

in speaking it sounds awful: One goes, one does, one reads, one speaks. *"When one is considering the alternatives"* sounds like it refers to someone else. *"When you are considering the alternatives"* sounds like the speaker is addressing me. Remember: as a listener I like the word *"me"*.

There is little danger in overuse of the word *"you"* in your presentations. Using *"you"* words sounds more conversational and entices the hearer to listen with heightened attention. The greater danger is to underuse *"you"* words, which could end up sounding like your speech is more like a paper prepared for a college or graduate school course.

When I taught university students, most of whom were in their early twenties, I allowed them three uses maximum of the hackneyed term *"you guys."* After the maximum was reached, their grade was reduced a notch each time they said *"you guys."* When I dine out, the waitress or waiter frequently greets us with *"How are you guys tonight?"* That is fine for waiters or waitresses and used once or twice it sounds personal. In a speech, it would be better to avoid the term *"guys"* as though you are trying to be a buddy to your audience. On the other hand, pepper your messages well with *"you"* words.

Four: Any method of delivery is okay except for reading your manuscript. Which is the most effective method of delivery? Here are three keys: 1) it's not the method. 2) it's not the method. 3) it's not the method. There is no magical method, no secret formula and no one single correct way. Some presentations are charismatic, funny, entertaining, enlightening, motivational, inspiring, or moving. Others are matter of fact, informative, educational, instructive or enlightening. The best method of delivery is what works best for you and suits you.

14

You are well-served to experiment and find the method that fits you best. Except one: reading. Do not read a speech. Reading a work meant to be spoken is the most deadly of all methods. There is nothing wrong with practicing your message so many times that you do not really need the manuscript except as a point of reference. Then, you will not be dependent upon your manuscript and can focus upon the delivery to an audience waiting to be led by you.

A classic study in educational psychology set up an experiment to determine how much an audience PERCEIVES it is learning. In the audience were a few hundred graduate level students. The speaker for the control group was an actual scholar who gave a lecture, primarily reading from notes. His content revealed actual groundbreaking content. The speaker for the experimental group was an actor decked out with phony credentials from non-existent schools, and phony publications from journals which were a figment of the imagination. His message overflowed with contradictions, false information, use of double talk, jargon, neologisms, phony statistics and inaccurate data. However, the actor was winsome, humorous and appeared to speak extemporaneously without notes. He exuded charisma, oozed an attractive personality and possessed a twinkle in his eye and a gleam in his smile.

Afterward, the listeners were invited to rate each lecture. Overwhelmingly, the audience felt it had learned more from the entertaining actor. The actor had fooled the entire audience of graduate students into thinking they had learned more and they enjoyed it too. None discovered the ruse. The outcome of this experiment is not to encourage public speakers to dazzle with mere charisma, but the effects were clear: speakers who use humor, who are not tethered to notes and who connect well with their audience will be perceived as the most effective and even the most credible.

The study also made clear: those who read from the podium or podium will be perceived as less effective... or ineffective. Whether you use a manuscript, cards, an outline or memory, use what suits you best. Any method is acceptable, except reading from notes.

Five: Eye contact is greater than the points you want to make.
Make eye contact with your listeners. Glancing up from your manuscript for a millisecond to stare into middle distance does not count as eye contact. Looking at no one in particular is not eye contact. Even a fleeting peek at an individual hardly rates. When you are in an audience, don't you enjoy it when the speaker looks at you, sees you, and then you feel like you are connecting personally?

Remind yourself to linger. Linger awhile on one person's eyes and then move to another and tarry for a while, looking at them while you speak. Even if you linger on a listener only once or twice, they will feel seen. Noticed. Connected. How long is a lingering gaze? It is more than a second or two. Practice lingering eye contact the next time you speak. Lingering too long can make the other feel uncomfortable, as though you are drilling down on them. Five or six seconds seems a good length. Then, your listeners will perceive that you are speaking to them personally, they will believe they are learning more and they will form a bond with you as a person rather than as a talking head who talks AT his or her listeners.

Draw reminder graphics to yourself on your manuscript or outline to signal where eye contact is most needed. When I felt it was especially important to be looking at the audience rather than at notes, I drew a pair of eyes on the margin of my notes.

Another margin note I find helpful is to draw a pair of eyes with the mathematical *greater than* symbol followed by a few dots, representing the points I want to make: $oo > ...$ That reminded me that my eye contact is greater than the exact points I intended to make. That was difficult for me because I try to write in an organized way and want to make my points clear. The reality is, they are not going to remember all my points but they will remember that they felt seen. That evolves into the perception, accurate or not, that they learned something or gained a new perspective. Eye contact is greater than making all the points.

Six: Prepare one hour for each minute of the message.
That is the norm. Perhaps it is not as daunting as it sounds. Preparation includes

struggling for the right idea and approach to the message; reading, study and research; outlining, drafting, rewriting and editing; practicing out loud; and delivery. It is possible you will invest even more than an hour for each minute of the speech, especially when your audience expects the highest quality from you.

Speaking uses every ounce of creative energy you possess and then some. Public Speaking is also a most satisfying opportunity. Crafting a creative work to help your listeners grow, learn or to be motivated is a satisfying way to invest yourself.

An experienced musician might play extemporaneously, to the entertainment of listeners. Most often, even the best musicians practice and rehearse for hours – much like public speakers. To improve at any skill or art, practice, practice, practice.

Rehearse your message out loud, four or five times if possible. Stand in front of a mirror, use an audio or video recorder or just practice it, but nothing prepares you better for the actual presentation than practicing out loud. Most important, practice out loud *on your feet*. Mimic as closely as possible the feel of the real experience of delivery. Practice the same time of day (e.g., morning, afternoon or evening) that you will deliver your presentation so that you capture the mood of the time of day. Pay attention to your non-verbal communication and to your use of pause, timing, and gestures. After you have practiced well, editing and cleaning up as you go, you will feel ready.

An advantage of the rule of one hour in the study for each minute behind the podium is that it forces you to keep your messages briefer. Perhaps you have heard the old adage about speeches: *If you haven't struck oil after twenty minutes, stop boring.* A twenty minute speech is long

for the audience to stay with you. Many of
the greatest messages are ten to fifteen
minutes long. A fifteen minute message is
hard to accomplish. It is far easier to write
a long message. To create an excellent
fifteen-minute work requires substantial
rewriting and editing, which is to your
advantage as well as to your audience's
delight. Few listeners have asked to hear a
longer speech and they most certainly
appreciate a tightly edited and well-crafted
work.

When you have rehearsed out loud a
number of times, you hit a point when you
know you are ready. In fact, you are eager.
You cannot wait to reach the podium and
begin. The excitement in your voice
becomes contagious as listeners can sense
you know where you are going and what
you want to accomplish.

If you are able to prepare your presentation
at least a week or more in advance, you
have the advantage of being able to

rehearse once a day prior to your delivery. There is no last minute panic or rush or worry about how it will come together.

There is a strange phenomenon experienced by public speakers. When you stand up and look into the eyes of your listeners, there can be a feeling of *"I just want to get this over with."* That could lead to rushing, which undoes all the good work and preparation you invested. Practicing a few times out loud and on your feet prepares you to relax, to avoid that *"get it over with"* feeling and to enjoy making your presentation.

Baseball great Yogi Berra said *"People don't want to hear about the labor, they want to see the baby."* Avoid the temptation to bore listeners with how hard you worked to research, prepare, write or wrestle with the topic. It's not about you. It's about them. Lift THEM up and embrace them, and you will have them listening to you on the edge of their seats.

23

Of all the suggestions or commandments about public speaking, perhaps this one should be first: Practice, practice, practice – out loud and on your feet. Total effort: one hour prep for each minute of delivery.

Seven: Edit the hell out of it.
First drafts are rarely that good and you are probably not the best editor of your work. It would be wonderful if you could get another to edit your work, but that is unlikely. And so, consider your first draft as just that: a draft. Research, outline, get it down on paper and then edit. Some of the greatest writers edit their works dozens of times. Author James Michener said *"I am not that good a writer, but I am one hell of a rewriter."* Oh that a speaker would care so much for the outcome that he or she would edit and rewrite.

Pianist Artur Schnabel said *"The notes I handle no better than many pianists. But*

the pauses between the notes -- ah, that is
where the art resides." With speaking, the
art is in the editing and rewriting.

Eight: A good message has a good
beginning, a good ending, and both close
together.
Invest the most time on your introduction
and the conclusion. Have you ever noticed
that people talk longer when they know the
least... or are the least prepared... or are
disorganized? If you grab your audience at
the beginning, they will follow you into the
rest of the message. A good beginning,
like a picture, is worth a thousand words.
Imagine hearing *"I'd like to tell you a*
story..." Your audience will lean forward
with interest to hear a story. Follow the
model of journalism: Many news stories
begin with a concrete example or
illustration. They tell a story about an
individual and then fan out with the
broader story. Start with a specific before
applying general principles.

25

Your conclusion should leave listeners wanting more, thinking, motivated, considering, inspired or at least glad they came to hear you speak. If appropriate, tie your ending to the beginning. When preparing a speech, finding the ending can be a challenge. When in doubt, always go up. Frequently the best conclusion already exists a few paragraphs up.

"...and both close together." Do not mistake quantity for quality. A well-educated audience will recognize good organization and will appreciate fine editing. If you labor to shorten rather than to lengthen your message it will show. Strive to bring your beginning and your ending closer together. A good message is always shorter than your audience's attention span.

Nine: Manage nervousness and use it creatively.

American's top fear is not the fear of heights, water, snakes, darkness or getting peanut butter stuck to the roof of the mouth. The #1 fear is the fear of public speaking. Emerson said *"Fear defeats more people than any other one thing in the world."*

The #1 antidote is to manage fear and to use it in your favor. Your listeners are glad they are not the ones up there speaking publically. When a speaker comes across with humility, listeners will cut you some slack and forgive your mistakes.

Know that even though you feel nervous, the audience does not know you are nervous unless you tell them. The biggest mistake you can make is to draw attention to a mistake or to your nervousness. Chances are high listeners will not remember a mistake even if they notice it. They are listening for your content and are not paying attention to your nervous stomach or shaking knees. Do not let it show. Do not draw attention to it.

Everyone gets nervous when they speak before a group. If you are not nervous, you could be in trouble! Speakers who claim to be *cool as a cucumber* are generally as thick-skinned as a cucumber and about as inspiring as a cucumber. The key is not to rid yourself of nervousness but to learn to manage nervousness for your advantage.

To be nervous means you care to do your best. Your nervousness will keep every nerve of your body focused on your listeners and on your delivery. Nervousness is nature's way of preparing you to meet the challenge. It keeps you on your toes, alert to your audience, thinking faster, talking more fluidly and speaking with greater intensity and enthusiasm. If nervousness shows in your voice or body, it is not a drawback. Your audience will have sympathy with you and appreciate your effort in the face of discomfort. Remember, your audience will not be paying attention to your nervousness or to mistakes unless you tell them.

Preparation and practice (out loud and on your feet) can reduce stage fright by up to 75%. Practice gives you the sense that *"I know it, I like it and I'm ready."* Practice helps you to maintain control, which feels good, and to even learn to enjoy speaking before a group rather than to wish to get it over with as soon as possible.

A well-known speaker was asked if she enjoyed speaking. She answered *"Before my speech, I am an anxious mess. During the speech, I am in agony. After the speech, I am completely exhausted. But to answer your question, yes. I love to speak publically."*

The #1 fear is not conquered by eliminating it, but by managing it and gaining control.

Ten: Use the "as if" principle.
This comes from Norman Vincent Peale, perhaps best known for his book _The Power of Positive Thinking_. Lesser known was the fact that Peale taught public speaking at a night school and that is where he developed the _as if_ principle: _Act AS IF, and that which you practice will tend to be. If, for example, you are fearful but want to have courage, act AS IF you did have courage and in time you will have courage. Similarly, if you are lacking in enthusiasm, act AS IF you were enthusiastic and your personality will begin to be just that._

Peale tells of an incident when he taught a class in public speaking. One student was completely desultory and uninspired in his platform presentation. *"You need enthusiasm,"* Peale said.

"I know," the man replied, *"but you cannot be enthusiastic just by wanting it."*

"Oh, yes you can," Peale insisted. *"Next time you speak, act really enthusiastic. Pour it on, give it all you've got."*

"That will be phony. You can't be enthusiastic just by acting as if you were," the student remonstrated.

Peale continued to encourage him to employ the *as if* principle. The next time he was the speaker, he really threw himself into his talk and the reaction of his hearers was electric. So inspired was this hitherto dull speaker that he continued to act *as if* he were the most enthusiastic of all speakers until in due course he honestly qualified for that category. To have enthusiasm, act *as if* you possess it and you shall have it.

31

In your speaking, act like you have
enthusiasm for your topic and your
audience will capture it. Act like you have
courage in public speaking, and you will
grow into it. Act confident and you will
truly become self-confident.

CHAPTER TWO: Connecting with Your People

When you speak, there is one person in your audience who will significantly benefit from your presentation. You will never know who or how you motivated them. Have confidence that you are making a difference. When you look deeply into the eyes of each listener, perhaps that is the one on that day who needs most what you have to offer.

The value of your preparation is multiplied exponentially when you connect with your listeners. Before you launch into your message, build rapport with your audience. Talk with them in a relaxed, informal manner. Bond with them. Like them and help them to like you. Relax and make small talk for a bit, as you might in a conversation. Do not rush to get down to business. The business will be wasted if you fail to connect.

Sizing up the Audience

Know your audience! Conduct an off-the-cuff audience situational analysis. Observe the audience to note about what you analyze about their situation. Consider the group's composition by age, gender, socio-economic status, cultural diversity, racial and ethnic background, sexual orientation, religion, group membership, political leanings, occupations represented, educational level, and interests such as sports, arts, travel, music and so on. Then consider how those factors might influence your choice of language. For example, in a group where 95% have no interest in classical music, illustrations about Toscanini or Heifetz might bore. On the other hand, speaking to managers about how to help difficult employees get along with one another might strike a chord that appeals to most of them. When you first see your audience, ask yourself: *what are my assumptions about this group of people?*

SIZE: Speakers can find a small audience more difficult than a large audience. A more formal speech that works with a crowd may fail with a dozen or two listeners. A chatty informal folksy talk that works so well with a small audience may fall flat with a large audience expecting a well-edited, thought-provoking presentation. Adapt your delivery to fit the size.

PHYSICAL SETTING: What will be your plan if there are distractions such as a baby crying or a cell phone ringing? If an obnoxious ringtone goes off, will you ignore it or acknowledge it? Sometimes it serves you well to acknowledge it kindly: *"That happens to all of us once in a while."* If you demonstrate a non-anxious presence with distractions, your listeners will relax and stay with you.

AGE: Focus on the audience's interests more than your own. Tailor illustrations to their age, not yours. If they are mostly the Medicare set and you are still carving out your career, speak less about relationships with bosses or co-workers -- your audience is not employed. If your audience is composed significantly of college-age people, illustrations about internships, networking, appearance, and careers will have more appeal than tips on how to apply for Medicare. People like to feel like they are learning about something that relates to them.

ASK THEM: You can learn about your audience by simply asking them... *"How many of you...?"* When I taught a class of university students, most in their early twenties, I asked them:
How many of you prefer CATS to DOGS? Prefer DOGS?
How many of you like SPORTS? Are not interested...?
How many of you are MARRIED? Have CHILDREN?

For how many of you was this SCHOOL
your 1st choice?
How many of you currently WORK 15
hours a week or more?
How many of you are NATIVES to this
state?
How many of you VOLUNTEER on a
regular basis?
How many of you love JAZZ?
CLASSICAL? COUNTRY? RAPP?
ROCK?
How many of you intend to become a
MILLIONAIRE in your lifetime?
How many of you are IN LOVE?
How many of you EXERCISE at least
three times a week?
How many of you are under some
STRESS right now?
Some of the questions were light, as a way
to warm them up to more serious inquiries.
After this ninety-second survey, I was able
to add more data to my situational
analysis: millionaire rated high, love less
so. They were driven to succeed. Most
worked part-time or more. More than half

volunteered. All were experiencing some stress.

I was speaking at a retirement complex where I had spoken before, but this time the listeners did not seem to be with me. They smiled politely yet appeared to be preoccupied and even distracted. Something was not right but I did not know what it was. Afterward I learned that one of their beloved members had died the evening before. They were grieving, mourning and looking for comfort and assurance.

What should I have done? Answer, which I learned the hard way: Always work the crowds for a few minutes before your presentation. Forget the grand entrance. Walk around, greet them and ask them how they are or is everybody okay today. This is the time to do a lot of listening, not talking. Touch them, shake hands, pat a shoulder or if appropriate give a hug. Make yourself highly accessible beforehand. Had I done that, I would have gathered information that would have helped me to shift the presentation to meet their needs that day.

Great public speakers are AUDIENCE-CENTERED. As I prepare for presentations, I have found it useful to close my eyes and repeat: *"It's not about me. It's not about me. It's not about me. It's about them and their interests. Not my interests.*

HONOR YOUR AUDIENCE. A simple exercise is to calculate how many "people minutes" are used in your speech. For example, if there are two hundred listeners and a speech is twelve minutes long, that is 2,400 minutes of cumulative time or forty hours. That tells me that my brief presentation is worth forty hours of my audience's time. I do not want to waste their time. I want to do my best for them. They hold high expectations of what they desire to receive which calls for high preparation and effort in content and delivery. However, if you consider that even an audience of one person is worth your best effort, you will always be well received.

Use of language in speaking
USE LANGUAGE ACCURATELY. Misuse of grammar, verb tense, slang, "*um's*" and "*you know*" and "*yous guys*" will cause an audience to disregard your ability to say much to them. Mark Twain nailed it when he wrote "*The difference between the right word and the almost right word is the difference between lightning and the lightning bug.*"

CHOOSE FAMILIAR WORDS. Build rapport with your audience. You do not want your audience to consider you long-winded, stuffy, ostentatious, self-righteous or a show-off.

FAVOR CONCRETE WORDS rather than the abstract. Choose the specific rather than the general. Give a single, specific illustration or story. Then, if needed, fan out from the specific to generalized applications.

EDIT TO ELIMINATE CLUTTER. Make your writing as tight as possible. Omit needless words.

ELIMINATE EXCESSIVE USE OF PHRASES or superlatives like "*very.*" Employ your verbs do the heavy lifting. Active verbs power a sentence. Avoid overuse of the verb "*to be.*" While it is acceptable to use "*is,*" "*was,*" or "*am,*" edit to replace them with action verbs wherever possible.

CREATE WORD PICTURES. Appeal to the senses. Make your listeners smell the bacon cooking over an open campfire.

EMPLOY THE USE OF METAPHOR. A metaphor is a comparison, sometimes subtle, but does not use the word *"like"* or *"as."* With metaphor, one thing stands for another to illustrate a greater truth or mystery.

EXPERIMENT WITH RHYTHM. *"I have a dream,"* spoke Martin Luther King, Jr., as he mastered a cadence that musically delivered one of the greatest speeches ever given. Learn from him: couple rhythm with repetition to drive home the point which will be remembered. When Senator Margaret Chase Smith's name was placed in nomination for the presidency of the United States, she stood at the microphone and said *"I speak as a Republican. I speak as a woman. I speak as a United States Senator. I speak as an American."* A little use of rhythm and repetition goes a long way. Too much can be considered gimmicky.

Test your writing for clarity

You will connect best with your people when your message is clear and understandable. A simple test has been devised to determine the approximate grade level required to read a passage. For example, the _New York Times_ is written at approximately the ninth grade reading level. So are many college textbooks. Many local newspapers are written at about the seventh or eighth grade reading levels. Professors may tell you that college freshmen typically write their papers on a grade level of twenty-five to thirty! Not good. What does that tell you? Good writing is clear and frequently concise.

The test is known as the _Gunning Fog Index_, designed to measure the readability of writing. Here is how the Index works.

Take a 100 word sample of writing and apply this formula: **FI = .4 (A+P)**

FI = the Fox Index, or, approximate grade level needed to understand the text. The result tells you how "foggy" your writing might be.

A = Average length of sentences (count words in each sentence and find their average). Divide the number of words by the number of sentences. For example, 110 words with three sentences would yield an "A" of 36.7

P = number of polysyllabic words of three syllables or more in the 100 word section. Words linked with dashes count as one word. Do not include names or common suffixes (such as *–es*, *-ed*, or *-ing*) as a syllable.

Add **A** + **P** and then multiply that number by **.4**.

EXAMPLE: Take the passage at the beginning of this section:

When you speak, there is one person in the audience who will significantly benefit from your presentation. You will never know who or how you inspired them. So, have confidence that you are making a difference. When you look deeply into the eyes of each listener, perhaps that is the one on that day.

The value of your thinking, research, study and preparation is multiplied many times when you first connect with your listeners. Before you launch into your message, build rapport with your audience. Talk with them in a relaxed, informal manner. Bond with them. Like them and help them to like you.

A: The section contains 104 words and there are nine sentences. Hence A = 104/9 = **11.6.**

P: There are **10** words of three or more syllables.

FI = $(11.6 + 10) * .4$ or $(21.6) * .4 = $ **8.64**

That means that this passage would require somewhere between the 8th and 9th grade reading level to understand it. Even though your audience may have more education than that, a lower Fog Index means it is easier to understand, hear and comprehend.

The index is an approximation at best and has limits. Not all complex words are difficult. The word *"relationship"* is not a difficult word although it has four syllables. A short word can be difficult if it is not a common word. However, the Fog Index can give you a rough gauge to reveal if your writing is clear and concise.

What should you do if your Fog Index is too high (generally higher than 12 for a diverse audience)? Answer: Shorten the sentences. Reduce the number of polysyllabic words.

While shorter sentences and fewer complex words applies to the written word, it is needed even more when writing for the ear. Winston Churchill said it best: ***"Short words are best and the old words when short are best of all."***

How to build your credibility so that you appear capable and trustworthy
A speaker's credibility rests in the perception of the audience. How do they perceive you? Are they accurate? Perhaps or maybe not. A speaker's credibility can be affected by the speaker's charisma, charm, sparkle, humor, smile, sociability, physical attractiveness or connectivity with the audience. A highly credible speaker may not be perceived as believable whereas a phony can win them over and fool them into thinking the speaker is trustworthy. Why do listeners accept one speaker's view and reject those of another? The audience might be won over by the speaker's evidence, convinced by the

speaker's reasoning or their emotions touched by the speaker's ideas, language, stories, humor, sincerity, style or delivery.

Some days that does not seem fair. One observer suggested that *"Leadership is 95% personality."* Perhaps that is hyperbole, but there is some truth to it. And so, employ the best tools in your speaker's toolbox to build your credibility.

GOOD ORGANIZATION is perceived as containing higher credibility.

LANGUAGE which is appropriate, clear and vivid strikes the audience as trustworthy. When an audience understands the message, they like the speaker.

DELIVERY counts. Prepare and practice, practice, practice. An old parody on speaking stated: *"Make them laugh, make them cry, make them feel motivated."*

SHOW CONCERN for the well-being of the audience. Establish common ground with the audience… what you have in common with them. Refer to their place, feelings, needs or interests. Listeners resonate to speakers who connect to their interests. These are the listeners who say *"I felt she was speaking directly to me."*

GIVE EVIDENCE. The Scottish philosopher David Hulme noted that *"A wise person proportions his or her belief to the evidence."* The perception of a speaker's evidence is what sways an audience to assign credibility and trustworthiness. Cite sources. *"According to the internet…"* fails to show credibility.

EXPLAIN YOUR COMPETENCE. Not boastfully, but tell about why your reasoning is credible. Explaining your preparation and research rates higher than resting on credentials.

GET THEM NODDING THEIR HEADS rather than shaking their heads. If you asked three questions and each solicited a negative answer, you put the listener in a negative frame of mind. Flip the coin: ask three questions that draw affirmation and that creates a positive mood. Never underestimate the mood of a listener.

SPEAK WITH GENUINE CONVICTION. Believe what you say. If you demonstrate enthusiasm or excitement, listeners will find your zeal attractive and contagious.

DELIVERY affects your perceived credibility. Steady and somewhat fast is seen as intelligent and confident. The audience believes it is learning when speakers use vocal variety which is lively and animated. Careful: loud can easily be perceived as untrustworthy.

President Harry Truman said: *"Sincerity, honesty, and a straight-forward manner are more important than special talent or polish."* Be yourself. Be aware of the factors which can affect credibility and trustworthiness. However, you will triumph when your sincerity, honesty and straight-forward manner strikes the minds and hearts of your listeners.

CHAPTER THREE: The Content

When you sit down to prepare a speech, teasingly remind yourself: *"If you can't make it good, make it short."* Of course you want it to be good. And short takes longer. It is easy to write long, unedited and sometimes wandering messages. Who said your messages need to be a certain length? If you want, tighten it rigorously. Who is going to complain? Most listeners will be delighted. So, partly humor and partly truth, if you can't make it good, make it short.

Every public speaking class ever taught started with this axiom:
Tell them what you're going to say.
Say it.
Then tell them what you said.

Do not keep the point of your message a secret. Do not presume your audience will get it. Make it clear: Tell the audience what is your point. Then summarize at the end to reinforce learning and the retention of your message.

The beginning
GRAB THE AUDIENCE. Ask yourself *"What is my Attention Getting Device?"* How will I connect with them and compel them to listen for more?

AROUSE CURIOSITY. Start with a question that relates to their interests. For example, *"How would you feel...?"*

TELL A STORY. When listeners hear *"Let me tell you a story..."* they lean forward to listen with interest.

BEGIN WITH A MEMORABLE QUOTATION. Shorter is better. Use a quote that inspires them to think or to nod in agreement.

HUMOR is a great lead if it works. If it flops, you risk losing their attention.

BEGIN WITH A SINGLE INCIDENT.
Mimic news magazines and newspapers.
Tell about one person's experience and
then apply it to more general applications.

STARTLE with a simple statistic.

REVEAL YOUR TOPIC. Do not wait too
long to make clear your point. Tell them
what you are going to talk about.

ACKNOWLEDGE OTHER POINTS OF
VIEW. Sincerely accommodate other
views, name them and give them
legitimacy.

CONSIDER NUMBERING YOUR
POINTS. If you have three points, say so
("*Three strategies for how to become…*").
Examine popular magazines and notice
how many articles offer numbered points
or bullets such as five tips, six myths,
seven strategies, four secrets, three

mysteries, eight top methods, ten
commandments, and so on.

KEEP YOUR INTRODUCTION BRIEF,
usually no more than ten to twenty percent
of the message.

AFTER YOU DRAFT YOUR MESSAGE,
return to the beginning to re-edit and tie it
together with the conclusion.

THE AUDIENCE IS WATCHING YOU
from the moment you stand up to speak.
Be careful not to spend the first few
moments arranging papers, water glass,
watch or fumbling around. Rather, start by
making eye contact with every person, take
a deep breath, smile, and begin with
confidence and control. Put them at ease.
Grab attention. A good start will help the
whole message go well because *"You got
them."*

The ending

It is hard work to end and to find a great conclusion, especially one that lingers in the audience's mind. Often a better ending is already in the body of the speech a few paragraphs up. When we do not really know how to end, there can be a tendency to keep on talking when an earlier ending would have been preferred. A common criticism of speeches is that they contained multiple conclusions and did not seem like they were ever going to end.

LET THE AUDIENCE KNOW YOU ARE ENDING THE TALK. Near the ending, slow down. Use more pauses. Change your stance, posture, pitch, gestures, tone or rhythm. Give clues that you are ending: in conclusion, to summarize, let me end by saying…

SUMMARIZE YOUR KEY POINTS to reinforce their understanding: Tell them what you said.

CONCLUDE WITH A BANG, not a whimper. End with a quote, a dramatic statement, a story or refer to the introduction.

NEVER TELL THEM they are bored or tired. This is a frequent mistake made by after-lunch speakers who tell the audience *"I know you've just eaten and would prefer to take a nap..."* If the meeting is running late, do not call attention to it. Assume people want to hear what you have to say. If you assume they are impatient because you are starting late, they will feel your anxiety.

PRACTICE THE CONCLUSION so that you know it well and can maintain eye contact, control of voice and management of the ending with a bit of firmness or drama. Practice the introduction and the conclusion most of all because those are the parts that stick in the minds of listeners. That is a fact about lists: people remember the first and last more than the content in the middle. Same with speeches: they will remember and appreciate your opening and closing.

DO NOT RUSH THE CONCLUSION. Make controlled use of pauses and silence. Slow down. Take a deep breath. After you have concluded, smile and make eye contact one last time before turning to sit down.

IT NEVER HURTS to say *"Thank you"* as your last words.

Organizing the body of the speech
Research of public speaking finds that people who heard a well-organized speech believed the speaker to be more competent and trustworthy than did those who heard the scrambled speech. Listeners will notice and appreciate if you are well-organized.

Organize first, write second. Consider the usual order for creating a message: idea, topic, purpose, point, research, organize, write, re-write and edit, practice, practice, practice. Numbering main points helps the audience to follow your progression of thought.

In public speaking, every rule is broken and often creatively, but first master the rules. Like abstract artists or jazz musicians, you can break the rules once you know what they are and why you wish to break them.

Following is a typical OUTLINE FORM:

Introduction.

Purpose statement.

Main point. Sub-points never stand alone.
Always have at least two sub-points.
Avoid too many levels of sub-points.

Second Main point. First sub-point.
Second sub-point.

Third Main point. Sub-points. The most
important points in any list should be the
first and the last.

Conclusion.

The purposes of public speaking
Speeches are used to inform, to motivate, to educate, to persuade or for special occasions like recognitions, introductions or celebrations.

NARROW THE FOCUS of your presentation. Broad topics are difficult to wrap your arms around. Observe how magazines headline their article titles or how skilled writers narrow their topics to create a specific focus. Writers err when addressing their message to everybody in general. You are best served to address your message to your specific audience and their interests.

USE PERSONAL ILLUSTRATIONS. Pepper your speeches with personal illustrations that could only come from you and no one else. Personal illustrations help you to connect with your people. *"She is one of us"* is the intent. They will know you better as an individual and appreciate that you too have weaknesses, faults, mistakes or funny things that happen to you. Avoid narcissism at all costs and use personal illustrations from the lives of others too, without intruding upon their privacy. A readership survey of newspapers found that one of the best read parts of the paper is the obituaries. People like to read about or hear about other people.

Speaking to persuade

Persuasion is subtle, sometimes subconscious, and emotional. You could be persuaded to do something or think something that is not in your best interest by a master at persuasion. Persuasion is used to sell, to convince, to motivate and to change ideas, values or attitudes.

At its worst, persuasion is capable of shading the truth just a bit, doctoring quotes to fit the position, choosing selective statistics, passing off opinion as fact, pandering to prejudice or stereotypes or playing upon emotions. We have been on the receiving end of the misuse of persuasion so we have a heightened interest in using persuasion with integrity and honor. Martin Luther King, Jr. said *"It is not possible to bring about a truly beneficial result by using unethical methods."* The ideal of effective persuasion is a good person speaking well.

HOW LISTENERS PROCESS
PERSUASIVE MESSAGES: Persuasion
is something a speaker does not TO an
audience but WITH an audience. Listeners
are all the while assessing the speaker's
credibility, delivery, supporting materials,
language, reasoning, emotional appeals
and non-verbal communication. Listeners
are arguing inside their own minds with
the speaker, engaging in a mental give and
take. The more directly the topic bears on
their lives, the more they engage in this
internal conversation with the speaker.
When a speaker hits upon their *"hot
buttons,"* they are engaged 100%. When
you speak to persuade, remind yourself
that listeners are holding a mental dialog
with you.

NEVER PRESUME THEY AGREE
WITH YOU. Have you ever been in the
company of a person who presumed you
agreed with them? They don't get it, do
they? They assume too much. That
dynamic alone can turn off those who are

undecided or still working on which position they favor. Speaking to persuade yields better results if the speaker presumes nothing about positions held by the audience.

UNDERSTATE. A speaker who overstates a position, fact or argument may turn off the very listeners he or she hopes to convince. Understating has the opposite effect. Listeners assign higher credibility to a speaker who is careful with facts and who understates a position. The audience may be more easily persuaded to consider a position which is understated rather than the one which is biased or partisan. Exaggeration backfires.

SKEPTICAL LISTENERS CANNOT BE CONVERTED unless you deal directly with their reasons for skepticism. Identify and name reasons why people might not choose your position. That is exactly what is going on in their minds anyway: thinking of reasons why to reject your position. If you already name some of those reasons, you will be credited with being fair and understanding the other side of an issue.

BE AS TOUGH ON YOUR SPEECH AS YOUR AUDIENCE WILL BE. Test it out in advance with a friend or family member who will provide a constructive critique of your arguments, data and appeal. Passion and enthusiasm for a position can be fraught with blind spots. Better to have a friend reveal your blind spots in advance than the ones you hope to persuade.

PROVIDE COUNTER-ARGUMENTS. Acknowledge that you know the other side's point of view. The more convincing you present the opposing positions, the bigger the bang when you provide an even stronger case for your own position. Great persuasive speeches begin with presenting counter-arguments so convincingly that listeners start to believe the speaker is actually arguing for them. Then, the speaker masterfully and politely explains why those arguments are insufficient. Present competing points of view fairly and then refute them.

IF YOU SLIGHT THE OTHER SIDE, you lose. Never attack another speaker. Attack arguments, not individuals. Even if listeners agree with your position, they will mentally dismiss you if you slight another.

YOU DO NOT HAVE TO WIN EVERY BATTLE. The goal is to win the war, not every battle. The goal is to persuade for a position overall. Do not require listeners to agree with 100% of every case that you make. Ask them to agree with your general position while acknowledging that they might still be working on some of the pieces and parts.

YOU DO NOT HAVE TO PERSUADE EVERY LISTENER. Baseball players do not bat 1,000 and neither will persuasive speakers. Be kind and gentle to those who

67

will not agree, but do not consider yourself a failure if you do not convince everyone. Therefore, narrow in like a laser beam on your target audience: who specifically do you want to reach most?

SHOW A NEED. Convince listeners there is a problem. The burden of proof is on the speaker to convince listeners that the old way is not working. Then present a plan for solving the need. Demonstrate why and how it will work. Show how a similar plan was successfully implement elsewhere. Or, if your position is to oppose a change or a shift, argue that change is impractical and that it will create more problems than it will solve.

VISUALIZE. Help your listeners to visualize benefits to them. Draw word pictures of what their lives might look like if they concur with the position you present. Use vivid imagery to show listeners how they will gain.

ACTION: Define what you want the audience to do and explain how. Conclude with a stirring appeal that reinforces their commitment to act.

As an accomplished public speaker, you have power to persuade. Use your power to effect change for that which is good. Recognize you have power when you speak. Use your power responsibly.

Speaking on special occasions
These are the everyday speeches you will
use to:
Speak to a service club,
Dedicate a wing on the local hospital,
Toast a friend at a wedding,
Honor someone at a volunteer dinner,
Eulogize a former colleague,
Introduce a guest speaker,
Accept an honor,
Present an award to a staff member,
Welcome visitors,
Report to the governing board,
Address employees,
Serve as luncheon speaker to a
professional organization.

Special Occasion speeches may convey
information or persuade attitudes, but that
is not their primary function. Rather,
Special Occasion speeches aim to fit the
special needs of a special occasion.

BE BRIEF. In most special occasions, listeners appreciate brief speakers. That does not mean that it cannot be a great speech. Make it your best work. You do not want an audience wondering *"When will he ever end?"* Better to leave them wanting more or appreciating how well you made a great point with brevity than to consider you long-winded.

FOCUS ON THE OTHER. Most special occasions are about another person or a group of persons. Talk not about yourself but about them.

RESEARCH FOR ACCURACY. Do adequate homework to get the facts right. I heard a famous Senator introduce another person and get the facts wrong about the person's background which made it obvious that the Senator really did not know the person. At a funeral I heard the eulogizer mispronounce the deceased person's name. If you cannot get the name right, how many other facts are likely to be inaccurate? Do basic research to learn the Who, What, When, Where, Why and How.

DO NOT OVERPRAISE THE PERSON. Overpraising creates expectations which are hard to fulfill or might embarrass the person.

USE HUMOR BUT only if you can. Anecdotes which are truly funny fit well at special occasion speeches. If they are not funny or if you are not good at humor, do not try.

WRITE IT WELL, prepare adequately, practice it and know it. A professor at a college was well known for his exquisite introductions of guest speakers. He spent hours researching, interviewing, thinking, preparing, writing, editing and practicing so that when he walked onto the stage, listeners knew they were in for a treat to hear his introduction of the speaker. Sometimes his introductions were better than the speech. Imagine becoming highly regarded by your peers for something as mundane as introducing another… or giving a report… or presenting an award. Make special occasion speeches an opportunity to shine.

SPEECHES OF ACCEPTANCE are well-served by brevity, humility and graciousness.

WHEN COMMEMORATING ANOTHER, find that person's unique thumbprint and tell stories about them rather than simply listing obituary style their credentials and accomplishments.

AFTER MEAL SPEECHES are light and entertaining. Do not tell listeners they are full and sleepy. Use short words, short sentences, few complex words, sharp imagery, vivid descriptions, colorful details or clever phrasing. Tell stories, give examples or share personal experiences.

73

IT IS ALL ABOUT RELATIONSHIPS.
Special occasion speeches are about people
and relationships. Knowing them and
connecting with your audience is greater
than a sparkling delivery. Make it
personal. Include names. Err in favor of
naming too many in the audience.
Demonstrate caring. Special occasion
speeches are about relationships, not style.

CHAPTER FOUR: The Delivery

CONTENT and DELIVERY are the two
parts to a speech. They are interwoven.
One is not more important than the other,
but neglect of one can ruin a presentation.
Have you not witnessed speakers who
invested almost all on the content? *"The
speaker was a nice man,"* they said
politely, *"but not very inspiring."* Or
consider the opposite: all sizzle, no steak.
A speaker can coast on charisma for only
so long. Balance your energy on both
content and delivery.

The voice of the speaker
Your voice is your tool. A pianist has a
piano, a carpenter has a hammer and the
speaker has the voice. Dissect the tool to
examine its components:

INTENSITY is the volume of the message.
Loud is used for emphasis. When
overused, it reduces credibility and turns

people off. Did you ever hear a message that was all loud? It makes you wonder *"Why is that person shouting?"* You stop paying attention. Soft is used to indicate an intimate connection or confidential information. People lean forward to listen attentively. All soft loses its effect. To control your voice and appeal to listeners, vary the intensity.

PITCH is how high or low the tone sounds. Changes in pitch gives the voice luster, warmth and vitality. The opposite is a monotone.

RATE is the speed. Speaking faster creates a sense of action. Speaking slower builds suspense. A speaker who speaks too fast all the time loses the listener. So does the speaker who speaks too slow all the time. The average speaker speaks 125 to 150 words per minute. Daniel Webster spoke at about 90 words per minute. Franklin Roosevelt, 110. John Kennedy, 180. Martin Luther King started his *"I*

Have a Dream" speech at 92 words per minute and finished at 145. Fast creates feelings of excitement, happiness, fear, anger or surprise. Slow is used for sadness or disgust, complex information, intimacy or to signal a transition or an ending. Do the math: if your speech is 2,000 words long and you speak at about 130 words per minute, you will need fifteen-and-a-half minutes. 3,000 words will require more than twenty-three minutes. Measuring your rate is an impetus to encourage tight writing and vigorous editing.

PAUSE and SILENCE. The Late Mike Wallace from the _Sixty Minutes_ TV news program was a master at controlled use of silence. He asked a question, the interviewee answered, and Mike would not respond but reacted with silence, perhaps with a slight hand or facial gesture indicating more was desired. Then the interviewee continued and that is often when the best parts were revealed.

77

Be intentional about pause when speaking. Use pause to give listeners a breather and also as an emphasis. Make a powerful point and then with the utmost of comfort, allow it to hang in the air for a moment. To listeners, pauses are brief. The same pause to a speaker can feel like an eternity until you demonstrate that you are comfortable and intentional with the silence. Mark Twain said: *"The right word may be effective, but no word was ever as effective as a rightly timed pause."*

TIMING. Look at comedians: pauses are critical to a joke or a story. Timing is a skill and an art form, which comes from practice, experience and attention to delivery. Allow extra time between points, paragraphs or after an emphasis. Timing is most important with the introduction and the conclusion.

ENUNCIATION is the clarity of the speaker's diction. It is well-pronounced rather than slurred. Many hearers delight in listening to a speaker with clear enunciation.

VOCAL VARIETY is to combine all the components of a speaker's voice in order to master the use of the tool for the pleasure of the listener. Variety of intensity, pitch and rate provides interest and adds spice to the delivery of the content.

WHEN USING A MICROPHONE, be natural. The mic is your friend. Kiss the mic. Use the mic to manage control and variety. A good sound system allows the speaker to talk with his or her people rather than to bellow at them. If you were speaking to a group too large but without a mic, you might find that all you could do was shout, which is a most uncomfortable arrangement. If possible, practice with your sound system so that you can manage its advantages to your benefit.

DO NOT BE DISCOURAGED BY
WHAT YOU CANNOT DO WELL.
Some of the most famous speakers in
history and today have had challenges
when it came to speaking. Abraham
Lincoln possessed a harsh and penetrating
voice. Winston Churchill suffered from a
lisp and a stammer. Bruce Willis, Julia
Roberts, and James Earl Jones were
stutterers. And then, there was Moses who
replied to God: *"I have never been a good
speaker. I wasn't one before you spoke to
me, and I'm not one now. I am slow at
speaking, and I can never think of what to
say."* (Exodus 4:10, Contemporary
English Version).

The key is not that a speaker suffers from a
speaking challenge but that he or she
overcomes it and learns to control the
voice. As Helen Keller observed
*"Although the world is full of suffering, it
is also full of the overcoming of it."* Lean
into your strengths and do not be distracted
by what you cannot do well. You have

overcome challenges in your life before
and you can overcome challenges when
you give a speech.

The body of the speaker
Actions speak louder than words,
especially in public speaking where non-
verbal communication can amplify a
speaker's message or contradict it. You
communicate subtle messages by your
posture, gestures, eyes and facial
expressions – sometimes without knowing
it, often not intended and frequently
misinterpreted by the audience. Heighten
your awareness of the power of the non-
verbal. Herodotus the Greek historian
grasped this truth: *"People trust their ears
less than their eyes."*

Consider the elements of non-verbal
communication:

POSTURE: When you are in a
conversation and lean forward, you appear
to be listening attentively. If you were to
slouch back with hands behind the neck
and staring at the ceiling, the other might
assume you are not paying attention. How
you stand behind the podium signals
listeners that you care... or do not care...
about your topic. Leaning forward
indicates increased intensity, especially if
coupled with a softer tone. Shifting your
stance indicates a transition. If intended, it
helps listeners know you are shifting your
points. If not intended, it distracts and can
cause attention to run off the rails which
can take a few minutes to get back on. If
you mindlessly stare out the window, up at
the ceiling or off into middle distance, you
come across as not paying attention to your
speaking. Leaning on the lectern suggests
a relaxed and informal moment. Doing it
non-stop suggests you are taking your
message lightly. Standing too rigid,
perhaps because of nervousness, can
indicate a rigidity of views. Practice your

82

message before a mirror to help gauge the effectiveness of posture on your delivery.

GESTURES. Gestures aid in getting the point across if used effectively. Otherwise, they appear amateurish. It is okay to talk with your hands if it is not too distracting. You want listeners to listen to you more than to watch you. Gestures are more likely to distract than enable which is why their use should be practiced and skillfully employed. Gestures should not draw attention to themselves or distract from your message but should appear natural and spontaneous (even though they are practiced).

DISTANCE. In conversation, how far away should you stand when speaking to another person? Answer: about an arm's length. Any closer leads to discomfort by the other. Further away and you seem distant. Removed. Likewise when speaking. What if you are high up on stage and your audience is sitting in the back rows? To you, it feels distant. Perhaps they like it that way. Notice how people talk about the speaker "up" there. Removed. Above them, literally and perhaps in other ways. Not on their level. Anything you can do to remove the distance and speak on their level will serve you well. If possible, come down to floor level... eye level... with your audience. If they sit in the rear and will not come forward, pick up the podium and move it closer to them. Or, if you can, forget the podium and walk to stand closer to them.

EYE CONTACT. Your listeners want to be seen. They want to know that you see them, connect with them and speak with them rather than at them. Maintain eye contact for about three-quarters of the time you are speaking. Less than that and you are likely reading your manuscript which is about the worst delivery a speaker can make. Let your gaze linger upon each person for a few seconds rather than for a fleeting moment. When you catch yourself quickly gazing up from your notes and looking at no one in particular or staring into middle distance, then you know you have some work to do on your delivery style. You want your listeners to feel seen.

MANNERISMS. One speaker jiggled the keys and change in his pocket for the entirety of his speech. That is what the audience watched. Another unconsciously groomed her hair and plucked lint from her jacket. Another toyed with his ear, as though to pluck wax out of it and then look at his finger. Yuk. Mannerisms can undo all the labor you invest in creating your speech.

PERSONAL APPEARANCE. Listeners see you before they hear you. They begin to form impressions about you before you even open your mouth. How is the audience dressed? Should you dress the same or more formally? It is usually best to err in favor of over-dressing than under-dressing. Your presentation is not a rehearsal. It is the real deal. Get a haircut, a good night's sleep, eat a good meal, bring some Rolaids and polish your shoes. How you look and take care of yourself counts to the audience. Dress the part. What would you look like at your professional best? Dress like you take your opportunity to speak seriously and as an honor. However, if you feel phony dressing up for public speaking that too will come across as a distraction. Whether or not we like being judged by our appearance, it is a fact that personal appearance is a part of the delivery. Notice politicians, how the jackets come off, the ties are loosened, the top button is unbuttoned and the shirtsleeves are rolled up. Does it seem phony? *"He is one of us,"* is the thought about making formal attire seem informal. Casual. Relaxed. In Control. Practice reading the appearance of your audience to suggest how your attire might communicate a message.

THEY ARE WATCHING YOU. Speakers
can err in thinking they are watched from
their opening line to their closing word.
Not so. The audience is watching you
from the moment you enter. They watch
what you are doing with your notes, with
your hands, with your water, with others
on the podium and with your eyes and
posture. They watch how you rise to
speak, how you approach the podium,
appearing calm, poised and confident...
despite how you really feel. They notice if
you immediately rush to get down to
business or if you take a few moments to
build rapport and acknowledge them.
They appreciate when you take it easy at
first, take a deep breath, smile and then
begin. Your audience is like a phone
which cannot be hung up. After you
conclude, they are still watching you.
They watch how you turn, how you smile,
how you sit and how you compose
yourself after a presentation that utilizes
every nerve and muscle in your body to the
point of sheer exhaustion... and yet still

look refreshed and in control. Do not get paranoid about it but neither neglect the reality that everything you do is a part of the message and has the potential to communicate.

Use visual aids

An average speaker who uses visual aids will come across as better prepared, more credible and more professional than a dynamic speaker who does not use visual aids. Public speaking research indicates that visual aids can increase the persuasiveness of a speech by more than 40%. Poorly done, it undermines your best efforts. When well-prepared and executed, it amplifies your presentation, your audience remembers it best and appreciates it more.

When I taught public speaking at a university, I emphasized two points: 1) Use visual aids at your own risk. If they fail, so do you. 2) It is usually well worth

the risk and you get extra points for
making it work.

PLUSSES OF VISUAL AIDS. Visual
aids enhance the clarity of a presentation
and make vivid your points. They add
interest as well as another dimension for
the audience to watch. Visual aids are also
known to help combat stage fright because
they shift attention away from the speaker
to the object being shown. Visual aids are
best regarded because they aid in retention.
People will remember your object lesson.
It stays with them. Making a presentation
where you present pro and con arguments?
Consider using two podiums or a white hat
and a black hat so the audience will easily
recognize the side you are taking.

MINUSES OF VISUAL AIDS. If not
done well, objects can distract rather than
reinforce the speaker's message. It can
appear gimmicky, even childish.
Generally, the plusses outweigh the

minuses. What can you lose? You have much to gain.

USING CHARTS AND GRAPHS. If you do it, keep it extraordinarily simple.

USING VIDEO with a TV recorder or a computer: a sloppy presentation is far worse than no visual aid. The audience wants to see you as a speaker, not as an equipment operator. *"This doesn't seem to be working today"* is never acceptable. If you have not prepared to do it well and double-checked every possible glitch, do not use it.

MAKE SURE YOUR AID IS LARGE ENOUGH. Holding up a small object which can only be seen by those in the first or second row will sink your ship. Words projected on a screen which cannot be seen viewed by those in the back row are wasted. Make it LARGE.

AVOID HAVING YOUR BACK TO THE AUDIENCE. Always face them, not away from them. When using a blackboard, easel pad or PowerPoint, if you are not facing your audience you are facing the wrong way.

DISPLAY THE AIDS ONLY WHILE TALKING ABOUT THEM. Do not leave the screen on after you have moved on to the next point.

TALK TO YOUR AUDIENCE, NOT TO YOUR VISUAL AID. The aid is just that: an aid to help you make your point. Be obsessed with your audience, not your objects.

USE POWERPOINT AT YOUR OWN RISK. When done well, it can dazzle. Usually, it is not done well. *"This was working when I practiced, but something is not working right now."* You lose. Or, the speaker forgot to pre-arrange with someone to turn out the lights or close the shades. You lose. Or, instead of a screen, the blank wall does not display the images well. Or, the audience sits and studies your entire desktop while you fumble to get it working, focusing all your attention on a keyboard and mouse instead of on your people. That results, of course, in no eye contact. Use of PowerPoint: high risk, high gain. If you cannot master it, do not use it.

Using statistics

Make statistics and numbers come alive to your listeners. Use techniques to help them grasp the broader concept.

LESS IS MORE. Too many statistics are a killer. Use sparingly.

BETTER TO UNDERSTATE. Do not acquire a reputation for exaggeration. When you understate, listeners will round up themselves.

USE "*GREATER THAN*" RATHER THAN "*ALMOST.*" It is a more powerful case to say that "*More than 60% of Americans are planning to purchase a new car*" rather than "*Almost 70 percent of Americans are planning to purchase a new car.*" "*More than*" trumps "*almost.*"

MAKE STATISTICS CREDIBLE and DIRECTLY RELATED to your point. Did you know that 57% of people in an automobile accident last year had eaten a pickle in the previous month? True, but not related or credible.

USE RELIABLE SOURCES. Would you trust tobacco companies to give you credible statistics on teen smoking? How about the AMA? The NRA? Lobbying groups contain obvious biases. Quote reliable sources to bolster your position.

THE AUDIENCE WILL NOT REMEMBER THE NUMBERS, BUT THE IMPACT LASTS. It is not important

that they grasp or memorize the statistics
you quote. Rather, make an impact with
them.

DEFINE YOUR TERMS. *"Average"* can
apply to a mean, median, or mode. Help
your listeners understand what you mean
by average. The median household
income in a town is $125,000 a year. The
mean household income in the same town
is $85,000. When quoting averages of
such disparity, define your terms.

MAKE IT PERSONAL. For example, if
talking about the divorce rate, count off by
twos and have every number two stand. If
you were all married, that is how many
marriages would fail. Personalization
drives home the point.

ROUND OFF. 71.976% means nothing
and is instantly forgotten. Seven out of ten
is remembered. It is not necessary to say
"about seven out of ten." The broad

94

rounded-off estimate is sufficient and well understood.

DOCUMENT YOUR STATISTICS. Where did you get them? The "*internet*" is not a credible source, although citing statistics from the American Cancer Society's website is credible and can be checked. Quote original sources wherever possible, even if obtained via the internet.

SIMPLICITY RULES. When using statistics, there are three key points: simplicity, simplicity, and simplicity. Keep it simple, understandable, and easily remembered.

WHEREVER POSSIBLE, FAVOR STORIES to statistics. Being with a story and work out from there. To begin with statistics is deadly. Instead, tell a story, and listeners will lean forward to receive your words.

Use inclusive language and recognized the multicultural composition of your audience

Use words that illustrate that you are sensitive to your audience's composition.

AVOID THE USE OF "*MAN*" when referring to both men and women. It is easy and inclusive to say *humankind* instead of *mankind*. While some may not care, most will be grateful for your sensitivity. Do not make all illustrations of one gender, but vary them.

AVOID STEREOTYPING jobs and social roles by gender. If illustrations about senior executives are male and illustrations about support staff are female, that indicates a speaker out of touch with current reality.

AVOID IDENTIFYING PERSONAL TRAITS THAT ARE UNRELATED TO THE TOPIC. A shooter on a college campus was headlined as a South Korean.

Why was that important to name? He was also a male, a twenty year old, a southerner, a college sophomore, a computer major, left handed, a member of the National Rifle Association, and bi-polar. Headlining his country of origin diminished regard for South Koreans.

PREFER NAMES THAT GROUPS USE TO IDENTIFY THEMSELVES. This changes constantly, but should you use black or African American or Negro or people of color? Should you say lesbian or gay or homosexual? Chinese Americans, Asian or Oriental? Native Americans, Indians, or first Americans? Use sensitivity in selecting descriptions of groups and choose terms that they prefer.

Rest to be at your best.
Scientists have discovered that the best preparation for public speaking is sleep. Sleep is better than cramming or over preparing. Get a good night's sleep. Take

97

a nap beforehand. Feel rested, ready and in control. Take no risk to become exhausted. A tired speaker will create a tired audience. Plan your schedule so that you feel rested, relaxed, ready and prepared. Those who prepare at last minute will be found out by their audience, who will not appreciate a lack of preparation, research, thought and practice.

Use your weakness
In college, I became a tutor for students in a public speaking course. This experience inspired me to teach public speaking at a university later in life. The professor assigned me to tutor a young woman with multiple sclerosis. *"This girl is going to fail,"* said the professor.

There was no way she could stand before a class and give a speech. She drooled. She had uncontrollable spasms. She could not keep her balance standing up. She was sort of a hunchback. She stuttered. She was scared to death, spoke in a monotone, and was very easily distracted.

People did not like being around her... their eyes avoided looking at her. After meeting with her, I did not see any way possible and was about to give up and resign the assignment. Then the inspiration struck about to make this work: USE YOUR WEAKNESS. Who in the world could give a better talk on what it feels like to live with MS than this young woman?

She and I worked hours a day on her ten minute speech. She would tell about MS. She was easily distracted. So, I would sit and listen to her speech and knock a pile of textbooks on the floor. I would yawn loudly. Once I even burped. I would stand up and go look out the window. I did everything I could to distract her, so by the time she gave her speech, she was made of steel.

In practice she read her speech in a
monotone. I went up, grabbed it from the
podium, ripped it in half and told her *Tell
your own story. Don't tell about MS. Tell
about what it feels like to have it. Use
your weakness. Tell about what you know*.

In practice, she still looked down at the
podium. I removed the podium and the
table. She had to stand there with nothing
between her and the audience. I would
walk around the room and tell her: *Look
me in the eyes the whole time you are
speaking*. She must have practiced that ten
minute speech for twenty hours.

The day came for her speech. She arrived
just as the class was starting. Her normally
frizzly hair was all made-up by her friends
in the dorm. She wore a professional
looking black dress, a string of pearls. She
was radiant. She felt good about herself.
She was ready.

When it was time, she walked to the front of the class, took a breath, stood up straight, looked every student deep into the eyes, smiled and told her own story of what it feels like to have MS. With poise and confidence, she poked fun at her spastic episodes and some of the nervous reactions she received. She explained the rejection, the looks she caught out of the corner of her eye, what it felt like to live in chronic pain and to always be fatigued.

They laughed, they cried, they relaxed and they learned. As she spoke, you could hear a pin drop, so riveted were they on her every word. Ten minutes later, she finished. There was total silence. Tears welled up in the eyes of her classmates and rolled down the cheeks of the professor.

And then, as though by silent signal, the entire class rose to their feet and applauded her with a standing ovation that lasted half as long as her speech..

101

Use your weakness and tell about what you know or feel.

Visualize yourself succeeding.
So much of public speaking is attitude: Believe in yourself. Believe that you can succeed. Take inspiration from a successful Roman leader who said: *"He can conquer who believes he can."* She can conquer who believes she can. A corporate CEO nailed it: *"If you think you can or can't, you are right."*

Booker T. Washington said *"Success is to be measured not so much by the position that one has reached in life as by the obstacles which he has overcome while trying to succeed."*

George Bernard Shaw wrote *"Some people see things as they are and ask 'Why?' Others dream things that could be and ask 'Why not?'"* Why not you?

Management expert Stephen Covey (*Seven Habits of Highly Effective People*) says: *"You can visualize in every area of your life. Before a performance, a sales presentation, a difficult confrontation, or the daily challenge of meeting a goal, see it clearly, vividly, relentlessly, and over and over again. Create an internal 'comfort zone.' Then, when you get into the situation, it isn't foreign. It doesn't scare you."*

He tells about Dr. Charles Garfield, with one doctorate in mathematics and another in psychology, who is a researcher in the study of peak performers. He researched peak performers in athletics, in business, and with NASA, watching the astronauts rehearse everything on earth, again and again, in a simulated environment before they went to space. One of the main findings of his research showed that peak performers are visualizers. They see it. They visualize it. They experience it

103

before they actually do it. They begin with
the end in mind.

A trapeze artist instructed her students on
how to perform on the high trapeze bar.
After teaching about what to do, she told
them *"Now, get up there and demonstrate
your ability."* One student looked up at
that insecure perch and he froze. Struck
with fear, he had a vision of falling to the
ground. His fright was so deep, he could
not move a muscle. *"I can't do it!"* He said.
The instructor put her arm around the boy's
shoulder and said, *"Friend, you can do it
and I will tell you how."* Then she shared
her trade secret. She said, *"Throw your
heart over the bar and your body will
follow."*

Visualize it. Picture yourself succeeding.
Imagine yourself speaking effectively,
clearly, and well as you connect with your
audience. Dream it, because, as an
Olympic gold medalist observed *"If you
can't dream it, you can't do it."*

Visualized yourself succeeding as an effective and dynamic public speaker and you will throw your heart over the bar.

CHAPTER FIVE:
Self-Evaluation Checklist

To improve what you already do well, evaluate your speech on the following items:

CONTENT
Topic appropriate to audience
Audience-centered
Clarity of ideas
Interesting
Quality of writing
Grammar
Creativity
Organization of points
Made points clear
Compelling counter-arguments presented, if persuasive message
Well-researched with sources cited
Use of humor, if appropriate
Introduction with attention grabbing lead
Conclusion

DELIVERY
Rapport with audience
Podium presence and appearance
Confidence
Control of nervousness
Pace or speed
Control of voice, inflection, modulation
Vocal variety, pitch, tone, intensity
Enunciation
Use of pause and silence
Use of props or aids
Delivered, not read
Personal investment of self in speech
Practiced adequately

NON-VERBAL COMMUNICATION
Eye contact (did eyes linger long enough?)
Posture
Appearance
Smiled
Mannerisms

OVERALL
Speech accomplished its purpose
Appropriate to audience

# # #

CHAPTER SIX: About the Author

John Zehring has a passion for communication as a speaker, teacher and author. His interest in public speaking began in college when his work-study job was to tutor students in a public speaking class. Later, he taught Public Speaking at Bryant University as an adjunct faculty member and has also taught Creative Writing, Administration, and Educational Psychology at other colleges.

A holder of three graduate degrees, John served for twenty-two years in the executive leadership of higher education. His role as a Vice President for Development and Institutional Advancement thrust him into speaking roles as the chief storyteller for his institutions. His writing led to opportunities to serve as a speaker to professional organizations, businesses, and community groups. Then, he changed careers and became senior pastor to United

Church of Christ congregations for twenty years in Massachusetts (Andover), Rhode Island (Kingston), Maine (Augusta), and as Interim Pastor (Arlington, MA) – a lifetime full of speaking publically.

He is the author of more than two dozen books and eBooks. His most recent book, planned for release by Judson Press in May 2016 is *Beyond Stewardship: A Church Guide to Generous Giving Campaigns.* Previous print books include *You Can Run a Capital Campaign* (Abingdon Press), *Working Smart: a Guide for New Managers* (Garrett Park Press), *Careers in State and Local Government* (Garrett Park Press), *Making Your Life Count* (Judson Press), and *Preparing for Work* (Victor Books). His articles have also been published in more than 200 magazines and journals.

John served as a consultant, a keynote speaker, a workshop leader, a professor and a director on boards of directors for

UCC Conferences in Massachusetts, Rhode Island and Maine. He was the founding editor of the publication *Seminary Development News*, a publication for seminary presidents, vice presidents and trustees (published by the Association of Theological Schools, funded by a grant from Lilly Endowment).

John is married to his high school sweetheart Donna and they have two children and five grandchildren. He lives in two places, in central Massachusetts and by the sea in Maine where he and Donna enjoy kayaking, skiing, snowshoeing, gardening, using favorite tools, taking rides, travel and most of all being with family, friends and neighbors.